SHEPHERD
MY
SHEEP

THIRTY YEARS AMONG
THE SHEPHERDS

by

Robert Gamble

AMBASSADOR

BELFAST ◆ **GREENVILLE**
NORTHERN IRELAND   SOUTH CAROLINA

Shepherd My Sheep

© Copyright 1997 Robert Gamble

First Published November 1997
Reprinted January 1998

ISBN 1 84030 001 9

Cover Photo: Exclusive Card Co., Edinburgh EH5 1RS

AMBASSADOR PRODUCTIONS LTD,
Providence House
16 Hillview Avenue,
Belfast, BT5 6JR
Northern Ireland

Emerald House,
1 Chick Springs Road, Suite 206
Greenville,
South Carolina 29609
United States of America

*To my wife Isobel
who has been my 'True Help Meet'
since our marriage on 22nd October, 1954*

Proverbs 31 v 28

Contents

❖

ACKNOWLEDGEMENT

I wish to thank my esteemed friend and brother in the Lord,

Mr. David MacLean

*for his encouragement and guidance during the production
of this book and for the time he spent proof reading the text.*

Foreword

❖

This is the book for which I have waited many years!
Delighted and stimulated by the vivid 'sheep' stories of my
lifetime friend, Robert Gamble, I have long urged a wider
audience. His many years as the representative of a world
renowned company dealing with the veterinary and pharma-
ceutical products needed in sheep farming has given him a
wealth of knowledge and experience amongst the sheep farms
of Scotland. Familiar, on a day-to-day basis, with the all round
care of sheep and particularly the ills that afflict them, the skills
of the shepherds and the problems posed to the veterinary
surgeons, he is ideally equipped to use these experiences in
the illustration of spiritual lessons. This book is the result of a
working lifetime amongst sheep and shepherds.

Entertaining and fascinating as the stories are, it is the
spiritual lessons drawn from them which gives value to this
little book. Believers pictured as 'sheep' is a familiar New

Testament concept, as Peter wrote:- 'For ye were as sheep going astray but are now returned to the Shepherd and Bishop of your souls' (1 Peter 2 v 25). For these sheep Christ gave His life (John 10 v 11) and they are now in the care of the under-shepherds (1 Peter 5 v 1-2) until the final 'tally' is made before the Chief Shepherd at the Judgement Seat. From the world of sheep and their shepherds our brother has drawn fresh lessons and has given fresh insights which illustrate and illuminate the allusions of Scripture.

I can recommend this little book most highly and can only trust that others will draw from it something of the spiritual help that I have gained from the experiences and stories of our brother over the years. It is my prayer that it may be blest by the Lord to the instruction of His people and to encourage those with a 'shepherd-heart' in the care of the saints 'to feed the church of God which He hath purchased with His own blood' (Acts 20 v 28).

Jim Allen
February 1997

Introduction

❖

A friend of mine, who owned a large hill-sheep farm in Scotland, was one day making his way to the top of the hill on his farm, accompanied by his shepherd, when the shepherd stopped and said, 'Sir, luk ahin ye.' (Sir, look behind you). 'Why do you wish me to do that?' he replied. 'Well Sir, ye'll aye see mair lukin back than ye dae lukin furrit.' (Well Sir, you will always see more looking back than you do looking forward). How true are the words of the shepherd in the experience of life. Those of us who are approaching the top of the hill can always see so much more in retrospect than ever we could in prospect. As another has said, 'Hindsight is a very exact science.'

With this in mind, I have been encouraged by some friends to look back and put on record some personal experiences and observations which I have made during more than thirty years of involvement with shepherds and their flocks.

In my earlier days, I was appointed as a field representative with a very well known company, whose products were produced exclusively for use by sheep farmers. I am thankful that the training I received with the company was a broad based one, covering not only the subject of sheep farming, but also dealing with agricultural and veterinary matters. This training was constantly being updated by means of input from our own technical advisers and through external seminars given by outside agencies. Naturally, I was most anxious to gain first hand knowledge and experience of the noble art of shepherding. I therefore took every opportunity available to give assistance at various 'gatherings', such as dipping, shearing and the many other times when the sheep were being attended to. In this way I learned practically how products were being used and the benefits which could be achieved by good husbandry.

I also obtained a useful publication by the Department of Agriculture for Scotland entitled 'The Shepherd's Guide to the Prevention and Control of the Diseases of the Sheep'. This book was published in 1958 and was dedicated to:- 'THE MOST ANCIENT - THE SHEPHERD'S - CALLING. Genesis, 4 v 2.' The information contained therein regarding ectoparasites, functional disorders and good management was most instructive, much of which is still being put into good effect by shepherds today as they tend their flocks.

Over the years my knowledge did slowly improve, but never at any time did I develop the expertise and knowledge of sheep which so many of the shepherds seem to possess, as a natural ability, from their youth.

During my time on the field, I visited sheep farms, sheep shows and sheep sales, all of which were regular events in many parts of the country. In the later years of business life, I was involved with various research projects from time to time, which brought me into contact with many of the well known Research and Development Institutes. I found their scientists to be a most fascinating group, wholly dedicated to research in animal health and welfare.

It certainly was a most interesting occupation in which to be involved commercially, and it also stimulated my interest in the many facets of sheep and shepherding which we read of throughout the Bible, from the early book of Genesis until the last book of Revelation.

With both of these interests and activities coinciding, it has been my pleasure, on many occasions, to share secular observations, with spiritual applications, at many gatherings of the Lord's people. Consequently, I now wish to put some of them into print, not in an endeavour to project my own limited knowledge of sheep farming, but only to illustrate the detailed instructions as found in Psalm 23, given for guidance to spiritual shepherds, which may not be so apparent to those who have no knowledge of sheep.

David was the shepherd who played his harp and sung these delightful Psalms while alone on the Judean hillside; his was just the experience of a shepherd writing about the Shepherd, drawing from personal experience, and communicating to us many truths, which have been a blessing and comfort to multitudes of the flock of God over succeeding generations.

'The sweet psalmist of Israel' was how Samuel described him as he recorded the last words of David (2 Samuel 23 v 1). On the Day of Pentecost, (Acts 2 v 29-30) Peter reminded his audience that David was also a patriarch and a prophet.

Today we still revel in the sweetness of the psalmist, the wisdom of the patriarch and the wonder of the prophet as he unfolds to us the glories of Christ in His life, death, resurrection and coming glory, when shall be fulfilled the words of David concerning his Lord:-

'The LORD said unto my Lord, Sit thou at my right hand, until I make thine enemies thy footstool.'

Many other Old Testament Prophets have also written on the subject of the shepherd and his flock:-

Moses recorded that he forsook Egypt and kept the flock of Jethro his father in law in the back side of the desert (Exodus 3 v 1).

Isaiah wrote:- 'He shall feed His flock like a shepherd: he shall gather the lambs...' (Isaiah 40 v 11).

Ezekiel warned:- 'I am against the shepherds; and I will require my flock at their hand' (Ezekiel 34 v 10).

While travelling on the road to Emmaus, the Lord gave His confirmation to the records of the Old Testament writers: '... That all things must be fulfilled, which were written in the law of Moses, and in the prophets, and in the psalms, concerning me' (Luke 24 v 44).

While many may have written of the gracious art of shepherding, the Lord said in John 10:-

'I AM the Good (beautiful) Shepherd'. All that was ever written about shepherds in the past has now been fulfilled in Me. The title He uses is that of the great 'I AM'; that which God introduced to Moses when he said, 'I AM hath sent thee' (Exodus 3 v 14).

It is interesting to observe how each verse of Psalm 23 is paralleled in the delightful comparisons of John in chapter 10 as he writes his Gospel:-

1. I AM the Good Shepherd, and know my sheep, and am known of mine. (v 14).

2. I AM the door: by me if any man enter in, he shall be saved, and shall go in and out, and find pasture. (v 9).

3. He calleth His own sheep by name and leadeth them out. (v 3).

4. And when He putteth forth His own sheep, He goeth before them, and the sheep follow Him: for they know His voice. (v 4).

5. Because I lay down my life, that I may take it again. (v 17).

6. And there shall be one fold, and one Shepherd. (v 16).

May we be guided by His Spirit to have both the Scriptures and our understanding opened to us, knowing that:-

'All Scripture is given by inspiration of God, and is profitable for doctrine, for reproof, for correction, for instruction in righteousness: That the man of God may be perfect, throughly furnished unto all good works' (2 Timothy 3 v 16-17).

Kenneth S. Wuest, in his word studies in the Greek New Testament, gives most helpful instruction on this verse i.e.

ALL SCRIPTURE:	Every writing of the Old Testament prophets.
INSPIRATION :	God - breathed.
DOCTRINE :	Teaching material.
REPROOF :	To rebuke or bring to conviction.
CORRECTION :	Restoration to an upright state, improvement of life or character.
INSTRUCTION :	The whole training and education.
PERFECT :	Special attitude for given use.
THROUGHLY :	Complete.
FURNISHED :	Fitted out.

Translation:-

Every Scripture is God - breathed, and is profitable for teaching, for conviction, for correction, for training with respect to righteousness, in order that the man of God may be complete, fitted for every good work.

Therefore, we learn from the teaching of the Lord in John 10, and from the apostle Paul, that the truth concealed in the Old Testament is revealed in the New Testament.

It is my sincere desire that the scriptural instruction contained in this book, coupled with the secular examples, will be thought provoking both to the spiritual flock and to those who have been called of God to ... 'Watch over your souls, as they that must give the account ...' (Hebrews 13 v 17).

Psalm 23

~ *A Psalm of David* ~

1 *The Lord is my shepherd; I shall not want.*

2 *He maketh me to lie down in green pastures: he leadeth me beside the still waters.*

3 *He restoreth my soul: he leadeth me in the paths of righteousness for his name's sake.*

4 *Yea, though I walk through the valley of the shadow of death, I will fear no evil: for thou art with me; thy rod and thy staff they comfort me.*

5 *Thou preparest a table before me in the presence of mine enemies: thou anointest my head with oil; my cup runneth over.*

6 *Surely goodness and mercy shall follow me all the days of my life: and I will dwell in the house of the Lord for ever.*

'Jehovah'

~ *Titles in Psalm 23* ~

V 1   JEHOVAH - ROHI
       The Lord is my Shepherd

V 2   JEHOVAH - JIREH
       The Lord will provide

V 3   JEHOVAH - ROPHECA
       The Lord that healeth

V 4   JEHOVAH - SHAHMMAH
       The Lord is there

V 5   JEHOVAH - NISSI
       The Lord is my banner

V 6   JEHOVAH - SHALOM
       The Lord send peace

Chapter One

My Shepherd

PSALM 23

❖

JEHOVAH - ROHI
The Lord is My Shepherd

❖

Verse One
The Lord is my Shepherd; I shall not want

AN EASTERN SHEPHERD

THE PEACE GARDEN - ELGIN SCOTLAND

Chapter One

ℳY 𝒮HEPHERD

PSALM 23 VERSE ONE
The Lord is my Shepherd; I shall not want

---- ❖ ----

Among the many descriptive titles of Jehovah which are recorded for us in the Old Testament, David now introduces us to:-

'JEHOVAH - ROHI : JEHOVAH MY SHEPHERD'

There is no doubt that this was a subject very close to his heart.

The prophet Samuel had visited the house of David's father, Jesse, to anoint one of Jesse's sons to be the future king (1 Samuel 16). As each son passed before him, the voice of God said: 'Neither hath the Lord chosen these' until all the sons, from Eliab downward, were eliminated. 'Are here all thy sons?' asked the prophet. Jesse replied: 'There remaineth yet the least, and, behold, he keepeth the sheep'. David was then brought in and the voice of the Lord said: 'Arise, anoint him: for this is he'.

It is worthy of note, that while the elder brothers were rejected by the prophet Samuel in chapter 16, and all followed Saul to the battle in chapter 18, David returned from following Saul to feed his father's sheep in Bethlehem.

In later life, the prophet Nathan reminded him of the words of the Lord (2 Samuel 7 v 8): 'I took thee from the sheepcote, from following the sheep, to be ruler over my people Israel'. So, from the early day of his anointing, until the end of his lifetime, David would recall the time spent tending his father's flock.

Thus, our experience in life, under God's direction, should fit us for the service that God would have in mind for us in future life.

It is only a man who has spent time with the flock that is able to understand and really know the state of health of each and every individual 'sheep' under his care, whether it be in the natural world of sheep farming or in the spiritual application of caring for the Christians in the local church.

As we peruse the Psalm, it would appear that David is looking back over life, firstly in retrospect to his youth, and then in prospect to old age and even beyond life itself. In verses 1-3 he is speaking about the Shepherd: 'I shall not want'. From verse 4 it is to the Shepherd: 'I will not fear: thou art with me'. It is good to speak to others about the work of the Shepherd whom we have come to know, but even better to be on speaking terms with Him in a personal way.

This confidence which David expresses in JEHOVAH - ROHI is a confidence in a personal Shepherd who knows, loves and cares about him. David's words in verse 1, 'I shall not want' reveal his faith in a Shepherd who will never leave him desolate. David will always have fullness of protection and plentiful provision.

I am aware that many of the incidents, drawn from my personal experience, which I shall refer to, are far removed geographically from the eastern setting, but they do serve to demonstrate that, even in a western climate and with commercial sheep farming, a very special relationship develops between shepherds and their flocks, and also between the sheep and their shepherds. This is an intimate bond that is unknown to those who have little or no knowledge of sheep.

Since there is still such a rapport in evidence, even in large flocks, how much closer it must have been with small eastern flocks, as the sheep even provided the shepherds with milk on a daily basis.

It is of little wonder, that in times of stress and difficulty, David would look back with fondness to his days of secret communion, enjoyed with his own flock, and with 'JEHOVAH - ROHI'. These were personal moments, when, alone with Him in the hills of Bethlehem, he learned to trust his life implicitly to Him. It was during these occasions that he derived such personal strength and courage, only revealed to us when he said to Saul: 'Thy servant kept his father's sheep, and there came a lion, and a bear, and took a lamb out of the flock: And I went out after him, and smote him, and delivered it out of his mouth: and when he arose against me, I caught him by his beard, and smote him, and slew him. Thy servant slew both the lion and the bear. ' With this assurance, he said to Goliath, 'This day will the Lord deliver thee into my hand' (1 Samuel 17 v 34-37 & 46).

This kind of confidence involves a two way communication process - between Shepherd and sheep and likewise between sheep and Shepherd.

Just overlooking the bonnie banks of Loch Lomond, which are well known from the refrain of the famous Scottish ballad 'By yon bonnie banks and by yon bonnie braes', there is a farm, where I often gave assistance at the 'Gathering's'.

On one occasion, after our usual discussion regarding business matters, Ian, the shepherd, intimated that he was going to feed the sheep and asked me if I would like to join him. I agreed, and together we walked over the fields and climbed the fences, until we reached the field in which were kept a large number of ewes, feeding, with their little lambs at foot. During our trek, Ian was carrying a heavy bag of ewe and lamb nuts and, as a matter of course, I offered to assist him, and was carrying the bag on my shoulder as we made our way towards the feeding troughs. When we drew near, the sheep scattered in every direction with lambs hard on their heels. What confusion and noise! Ewes and lambs all mixed up together and bleating for all they were worth. Ian looked at me in rather an apologetic way and said: 'There is something wrong today.' 'Is it me?' I asked. 'Yes, the sheep don't know you!'

Here I was, carrying a bag, full of their favourite feed; but they would not take it from me because I was a stranger to them.

I immediately handed over the feed and withdrew a little, only to see that they almost knocked the shepherd over in their excitement. I watched with delight to see the confidence and trust which they had in the man who was their shepherd.

We must never assume that sheep are stupid animals, because they are not, and, in certain circumstances, they have a natural intuition that even excels their keepers.

I once visited a very remote area of West Perthshire, which was many miles from the main roads, a combined sheep farm and shooting lodge for red deer. It was rather a wintry day with a little snow falling. I was greeted in rather a strange manner by Frank, who was the stalker / shepherd. As he opened the door of his home he said: 'You're no fiert (afraid) tae come in here the day! But in ye come - you are aye welcome to hae yir dinner (have a meal with us) but it's up to you!'

This greeting rather took me by surprise, as he was not the type to raise an alarm unnecessarily. 'What would your advice be?' I asked. Silently, he raised his binoculars and scanned the mountains for a time; after which he handed them to me. 'Have a look yourself,' he said. 'Tell me what to look for,' I replied. 'Just watch the sheep and you'll see for yourself.'

What a sight met my gaze as I stood there scanning the mountain tops. Snow was now falling heavily and sheep were running as fast as they could from the tops, in single file, down the mountain tracks. There were scores of them, fleeing as though they were being chased by dogs. 'A very bad sign,' said Frank. So, without a moment's delay, I made a hasty retreat out of the farm track, glad to be back to the main road and civilisation again.

I was most grateful for such an accurate weather report from the sheep, as the house and the road into it was completely blocked with snow drifts for the next two weeks. With no one aware of my location, and no telephone or vehicle access available, it would have caused some anxiety as to my safety.

Another visit I made, to a different location, illustrated to me the words of the Lord in John 10 v 3 '... and the sheep hear his voice: and he calleth his own sheep by name.'

Tammie, (as he was affectionately known) was a crofter who lived in the far north of the Shetland Islands. One day, he kindly invited me for lunch. Naturally, the conversation turned to sheep. I asked him if he could call his sheep by name, and he proudly said, 'Yes.' 'Would you please do that for me?' I asked, and he readily agreed.

We stood by the fence and he called them each by name. Alas - no response. I also called their names but no response! Poor Tammie; he did not like to tell me the problem, until I said: 'Is it me?' - 'Yes! They do not know the voice of a stranger!' he replied. They must have been listening to our conversation at the fence. I quickly hid in a nearby shed and watched through the window as the dear old man called them each by name. What a difference! They now came running towards him to lick his hand: it was almost as though they were indicating that they were glad that the stranger had got out of the way. How important it is for us to learn from sheep! They do not accept food from strangers or listen to their voice.

In the introduction, we observed the harmony of the Old Testament with the New, and linked the spiritual flock with the secular. It would therefore be in keeping to ask the question,

'How should shepherds be appointed among the Lord's people today?'

Some may say 'by committee'; others may say 'by ballot' or even 'by their C.V.'. What can we learn on this subject from a study of the inspired book?

The apostle Paul in Acts 20 and the apostle Peter in 1 Peter 5 both give us a threefold description of the men who are the guides: i.e. Elders, Overseers and Shepherds.

Paul writes:
Acts chapter 20

v 17   ELDERS   indicating   MATURITY

v 28   OVERSEERS   indicating   AUTHORITY
v 28   SHEPHERDS   indicating   RESPONSIBILITY
(Note: The expression of v 28 'to feed' means to shepherd.)
v 28   APPOINTED BY THE HOLY GHOST

Peter writes:
1 Peter 5 v 2-3
RE: ELDERS: OVERSEERS: SHEPHERDS.

Three negatives:		Three positives:	
NOT		BUT	
Constraint	(forced)	Willingly	(voluntarily)
Filthy Lucre	(base gain)	Ready mind	(alacrity)
Lords	(despotic rule)	Examples	(pattern)

From the illustrations of the shepherds that we looked at in v 1, we can note that the mature shepherd is acutely aware if the flock is being fed or if it is being scattered; he can quickly observe any movement of anxiety among the sheep which indicates a pending storm and he knows full well if the flock is responding to his voice, or if the sheep are keeping their heads down, as they always do with strangers.

As in the natural sphere, so it is with the 'flock of God' spiritually, with spiritual shepherds requiring to exercise the same vigilant care, discernment and watchfulness.

Chapter Two

GREEN PASTURES

AND

STILL WATERS

PSALM 23

❖

JEHOVAH - JIREH

The Lord will Provide

❖

Verse Two
He maketh me to lie down in green pastures: He leadeth me beside the still waters.

GREEN PASTURES AND STILL WATERS

FIRTH OF CLYDE

Chapter Two

$\mathcal{G}$REEN $\mathcal{P}$ASTURES AND $\mathcal{S}$TILL $\mathcal{W}$ATERS

PSALM 23 VERSE TWO

He maketh me to lie down in green pastures

❖

We may well ask the question, 'How do you make sheep lie down?' By jumping on their back? By harangue and harassment?

CERTAINLY NOT!

Such activities as these will only create distress and quickly scatter the flock hither and thither, causing them to lose their way and prevent their feeding, resulting in hunger and ultimately resulting in their death.

What does the expression 'He maketh me to lie down in green pastures' convey to us? How can the desired result be obtained?

The caring shepherd will 'create the condition' for the flock to lie down. Sheep will only lie down of their own accord, when there is tranquillity and freedom from anxiety. The phrase simply means 'a time of repose after exertion'.

How beautiful are the words of the Song of Songs 1 v 7: 'Tell me, O thou whom my soul loveth, where thou feedest, where thou makest thy flock to rest at noon.'

When the flock is well fed, at rest and ruminating, then they are really thriving. If they are being driven about for any reason, they will not produce milk or feed their young lambs, resulting in poor condition and stunted growth.

Green pastures are the fresh, young, spring grasses, which will be free of parasitic contamination and therefore produce good, clean, healthy ewes, which in turn produce strong, thriving lambs.

Such picturesque language from the Psalm does convey the scene: flocks lying at rest, beside the waters of quietness, contented under the watchful eye of their caring Shepherd.

How important, in the spiritual flock, to ensure that the flock is being fed on the fresh, green pasture of the Word with no contaminating or disturbing influence.

While it is imperative for the shepherd to 'create conditions' that are conducive to good health in secular life, there is an even more demanding task required of the spiritual shepherd, to ensure that the flock, which he leads, is preserved from external and internal problems, in order to create and maintain good conditions under which the flock of God will prosper.

v 2 HE LEADETH ME BESIDE THE STILL WATERS

David would have been taught about Moses, the man who led the people of Israel for forty years through the wilderness. How they tried Moses' patience as he passed through difficult paths, causing him great distress.

Note the words of Moses (Deuteronomy 32 v 2) spoken in order to calm a rebellious people and create an atmosphere of peace:

'My doctrine shall drop as the rain, my speech shall distil as the dew, as the small rain upon the tender herb, and as the showers upon the grass.'

The ancient proverb states, 'The best of men are only men at their best' and Moses, like many another, failed in what had been his strongest point.

'Now the man Moses was very meek, above all the men which were upon the face of the earth' (Numbers 12 v 3).

When the people murmured against him and his leadership continually, he came to the point where he lost his temper and struck the Rock TWICE calling them 'rebels'. As a result, he was not permitted to take the people over the Jordan and into the Promised Land. The seriousness of this action, of course, we understand when reading 1 Corinthians 10 v 4: That 'Rock' was 'Christ' and would only be smitten ONCE.

His frustration and weakness, on this sad occasion at Meribah, overcame him, and he did not display the features which the apostle Peter outlined ... 'ensample to the flock: a pattern to be followed' (Numbers 20 v 10).

God demanded the very highest standard of leadership from Moses because he was a type of the Leader that would come in Deuteronomy 18 v 15: 'The Lord thy God will raise up unto thee a Prophet from the midst of thee, of thy brethren, like unto me; unto him ye shall hearken'.

It must be said, however, that his outstanding leadership and passionate love for the people of Israel was displayed on many later occasions. His concern for them, despite their personal attacks, was so great that he said to the Lord (Exodus 32 v 32) 'Yet now, if thou wilt forgive their sin; and if not, blot me, I pray thee, out of thy book which thou hast written'.

When the Lord intimated to him that he would not take the people into the land of Canaan because of the Meribah incident, his plea was for a successor ... 'which may lead them out, and which may bring them in; that the congregation of the Lord be not as sheep which have no shepherd'.

Thereafter he took the young man Joshua and laid his hands on him, charged him and placed his honour on him. (Numbers 27 v 16-23).

It is so often a cause for concern today that many older men appear to be unwilling, either to delegate, or lay aside their charge, but hold their office until they are physically unable to carry on. It would ensure the future of any company if the young men received the same introduction as Joshua, because we do read 'And the people served the Lord all the days of Joshua' (Judges 2 v 7).

Perhaps the instruction to the Levites would give guidance:

Numbers	8 v 24	at	25 years	learning
	4 v 3	at	30 years	serving
	8 v 25	at	50+ years	guiding

In our Psalm, the shepherd is leading in v 2, and again leading in v 3. We should note that it is not exactly the same word that is being used on each occasion. The leading in v 2 is: 'a gentle guiding toward the waters of rest with thirsty sheep being satisfied at still waters'. Sheep will not drink or pass over running waters, as they are afraid of them, and therefore we see the importance of the Shepherd leading them beside waters of quietness. In the phrase 'He leadeth' in v 3, a stronger word is used, which we will consider later.

This is where the skill and local knowledge of the shepherd is so important, as he knows the needs and wants of the flock, and is able to lead them to the place where there are deep, still, cool springs of water from which to draw. Perhaps, like Jacob, he will require to roll away the stone from the well's mouth and water the flock, or even take them out to pasture lands to enjoy the sweet dew of the early morning before the sun arises. Water is an absolute necessity for the survival of life in the natural realm for both man and beast; it is used for refreshment, sustenance and cleansing. Without it, all flesh would die within a matter of days.

Isaac digged again the wells of Abraham his father; Jacob drew water for the sheep when he met his beloved Rachel. The Lord himself sat with a woman at the well, when the woman said: 'Sir, thou hast nothing to draw with, and the well is deep' (John 4 v 11).

Ephesians 5 v 25-26 reminds us .. 'Christ loved the church, and gave himself for it; that he might sanctify and cleanse it with the washing of water by the word.'
There are those that read the Word and say that it is rather a dry morsel, but it becomes evident that they are only scraping the surface.

We must 'DIG' wells before we are able to 'DRAW WATER'. As a boy in Ireland, I watched while workmen started to dig a well. It was hard labour and, working in a very confined space, they laboured single handed for many hours. At last they reached the source of the 'living water', which continued to flow, and, the more that was drawn, the sweeter the water became. Digging and drawing, from the well of the

AN ORPHAN LAMB

INTRODUCTION TO A NEW MOTHER

Word, can only be achieved and maintained by diligently studying, as Paul exhorts in 1 Timothy 4 v 13-16 '... give thyself wholly to them: that thy profiting may appear unto all'.

Stagnant waters can develop a species of snail, which becomes part of the life cycle of liver flukes, and they, in turn, can cause a fatal condition known as 'Black's Disease'.

Young lambs are particularly at risk from nematodes, which are picked up from the grass in spring time, with devastating consequences. It took many years for a suitable therapeutic product to be produced and the only preventative measure which a shepherd could take was to keep lambs on clean grass that had not been contaminated.

Peter, the shepherd, gives good advice to the flock in 1 Peter 2 v 2: 'As newborn babes, desire the sincere (uncontaminated) milk of the word, that ye may grow thereby'. Sheep of all ages are continually exposed to endo-parasites or ecto-parasites, so the vigilance and care of a good shepherd is imperative.

FEATURES OF A GOOD SHEPHERD

The prophet Isaiah (40 v 11) gives us the good shepherd's 'job description'.

- He shall FEED (guard) his flock like a shepherd.
- He shall GATHER (take hold of) the lambs with his arm, (strength/might/power).
- He shall CARRY (lift up) them in his BOSOM (love/ warmth/security).
- He shall GENTLY (carefully) LEAD (guide) those that are with young (nursing ewes).

Happy is the flock of God where shepherds are:

FEEDING, GATHERING, LIFTING, CARRYING, WARMING and LEADING.

When the apostle Paul arrived at Miletus, he called for those who were responsible for the church at Ephesus and said:

'Take heed therefore unto yourselves, and to all the flock, over the which the Holy Spirit hath made you overseers, to feed the church of God, which he hath purchased with his own blood. For I know this, that after my departing shall grievous wolves enter in among you, not sparing the flock. Also from among your own selves shall men arise, speaking perverse things, to draw away disciples after them.' (Acts 20 v 28-30).

The warning from the apostle is so salutary: 'From among your own selves.'

It was not to the sheep, but to the shepherds that the Lord pronounced the woes in Ezekiel 34 v 10.

I am indebted to a respected friend for an outline on the shepherds of Israel in Ezekiel as follows:

From the death of Josiah, after the battle of Megiddo (609 BC) the final years of the history of Judah were an unmitigated disaster and ended in the destruction of Jerusalem and the removal of the people to Babylon. Ezekiel is commanded to put the blame where it belonged - on those described as 'the shepherds of Israel' (Ezekiel 34 v 1-10). These shepherds of Jehovah's flock were the Kings who ruled during these years - even though they had not been appointed by God.

There were four Kings:

JEHOAHAZ, JEHOIAKIM,
JEHOIACHIN, ZEDEKIAH.

Appointed by men these shepherds brought disaster to Judah and are charged by Jehovah through Ezekiel in chapter 34 with:

1	SELFISHNESS	'they do feed themselves; should not the shepherds feed the flock?'
2	RAPACIOUSNESS	'ye eat the fat and ye clothe you with the wool'.
3	OFFICIOUSNESS	'ye kill them that are fed' 'with force and with cruelty ye ruled'.

Is it any wonder Jehovah says:

1 'Woe be to the shepherds of Israel'.
2 'Behold I am against the shepherds of Israel'.
3 'I will require My flock at their hand'.

The specific charges brought against the shepherds show the absence of any shepherd care in these terrible years before Nebuchadnezzar finally destroyed the city in 586 BC and carried all the people to Babylon.

The charges are as follows:

The DISEASED have ye not strengthened...:	WEAK
Neither have ye healed that which was SICK...:	WEARY
Neither have ye bound the BROKEN...:	WOUNDED
Neither brought again that which was DRIVEN away... :	WAYWARD
Neither have ye sought that which was LOST... :	WANDERING

Normal shepherd care was missing and both shepherds and sheep ended up in captivity for seventy years in Babylon.

It is doubtless against this Old Testament background that Peter instructs New Testament shepherds to guard and care for their flock, in order to prevent them being scattered in a similar way.

Chapter Three

Restoration

AND

Righteousness

PSALM 23

❖

JEHOVAH - ROPHECA

The Lord that Healeth

❖

Verse Three
*He restoreth my soul: He leadeth me in the paths
of righteousness for His Name's sake.*

NEGLECTED

PHOTOGRAPHED BY THE ROADSIDE

NOTE: FRONT SHOULDER   REAR FOOT
Broken fleece: parasitic infestation.   Unable to stand on it: chronic foot-rot.

Chapter Three

ℛESTORATION
AND ℛIGHTEOUSNESS

PSALM 23 VERSE THREE
He restoreth my soul

❖

To the layman, it appears that sheep can just wander around unattended, but nothing could be further from the truth. Sheep, more than any other domestic animal, demand constant attention; otherwise, the flock will very quickly develop a whole variety of serious problems.

Even now, as I drive around the countryside, I can see sheep in poor, unthrifty condition, with broken fleeces and bad foot rot. This causes much unnecessary pain and distress to the poor animals, and fills me with revulsion, as it is an evidence of neglect on the part of the owner and, indeed, is a legal offence.

'Restoration' means to restore to a former state. In secular writings, this word is used to describe the action of fishermen mending their nets and also the action of surgeons re-setting bones.

I asked a shepherd to tell me exactly what he did when he went to the hills. His terse reply was, 'Watch the sheep!'

Probing further, I said, "What for?' His reply, 'Everything!' 'Well then,' I said, 'tell me more about everything!'

Sheep are very easily 'couped' - an old Scottish expression to mean 'off their feet and on their back'. This can be caused by a variety of factors. When 'couped', the sheep are quite helpless to get back on their feet by themselves, or to restore their balance. In this predicament, gases build up in their rumen which can ultimately suffocate them. Alternatively, birds of prey often swoop down and pick out their eyes, leaving them in a distressed condition.

Some sheep can also become 'loners', straying away from the main flock; unfortunately, their lambs tend to follow their example, a sure indicator that they are either, sick, weak, hungry or diseased. When healthy, the preference is always to continue as an integral part of the flock. When parents are happy and content, children will follow their example, and this is so often evident in the experience of life.

Other sheep, that have been running too long on soft, marshy, dirty land, can develop foot rot. This is a very painful and debilitating problem, which soon affects their walk, prevents them from foraging for food, and, ultimately, leads to their death due to starvation.

These conditions, and many others beside, demand that shepherds maintain constant alertness when 'watching' the sheep. It requires immediate action to get 'couped' ones back on their feet and straying ones returned to the flock. It takes skill for the shepherd to use his knife and trim off the parts of the hoof that have been damaged by the invading bacteria. How important are the words of Hebrews 13 v 17: '... for they watch for your souls, as they that must give account.' Not only are shepherds responsible, they are also accountable. Jacob knew all about this when he was a shepherd with his father-in-law, Laban. He said, 'I bore the loss'.

In Psalm 42 v 5, David cries: 'Why art thou cast down, O my soul? And why art thou disquieted in me?' Just like the sheep he had been 'couped' - he was helpless, and in need of the Shepherd.

Whenever a sheep has been 'couped', it is not just a case of standing it up and off she goes. You must wait a little time for it to gain its equilibrium, restore its blood flow, and regain its balance and confidence once more. Otherwise, it will fall over again, unless time is taken.

In Christian life the task of stabilising one who has been 'couped' is often a painstaking, long term work which demands patience, understanding, support and much encouragement from the shepherds.

In modern parlance we say: 'An ounce of experience is worth a ton of knowledge'. No one knew that any better than David. He was well aware of the bitterness of soul that overcame him when he strayed from the watchful eye of the Shepherd.

A LITTLE EWE LAMB

The occasion in David's life which caused this trauma was at the time when kings went forth to battle (2 Samuel 11 v 1), and he stayed at home. Spying a beautiful woman named Bathsheba from the house top as she was washing herself, he took her and committed adultery with her. As a result, she was with child. Consequently, he arranged for her husband, Uriah, to come home from the battle for a home visit, in order to cover his sin. Although Uriah did return to Jerusalem, he refused to go home to be with his wife while the others were still at war and encamped in the fields. David then instructed his commander, Joab, to put Uriah into the forefront of the battle and, as a result, he was killed.

The Lord instructed the prophet, Nathan, to visit David and he told him a story about a very rich man who had flocks and herds and who was about to entertain a traveller friend. The rich man took a little ewe lamb from one of his very poor neighbours and he dressed it and killed it for the occasion. On hearing this, David's anger was kindled and he decreed: 'The man that hath done this thing shall surely die, and he shall restore four fold.' Nathan then said: 'Thou art the man.'

David knew the import immediately. A little ewe lamb like this would have been an orphan, reared as a pet with the children, eating the children's food and drink and sleeping in their bosom, just like one of the family.

How descriptive of his own behaviour with Bathsheba and Uriah.

The words of the Lord in Matthew 7 v 2 are:
'For with what judgement ye judge, ye shall be judged.'

David ultimately paid the full price: a four fold judgement from the Lord in the death of his own four sons.

Hear his pathetic cries in Psalm 51:

v 1   Have mercy upon me, O God...
v 3   I acknowledge my transgressions and my sin...
v 4   Against thee, and thee only, have I sinned...
v 12   Restore unto me the joy of thy salvation...

REPENTANCE BEFORE RESTORATION

v 17   A broken and a contrite heart, O God, thou wilt
        not despise.

We must be careful not to take a self righteous attitude in the matter of restoration, thinking that 'it will never happen to me'.

The apostle gives us a warning and guidance in this matter:
'Let him that thinketh he standeth, take heed lest he fall.' (1 Corinthians 10 v 12).
'Brethren, if a man be overtaken in a fault, ye which are spiritual, restore such an one in the spirit of meekness; considering thyself, lest thou also be tempted.' (Galatians 6 v 1).

On one occasion, two elders were delegated to visit a member of their company who had gone astray. As they conversed on the way, one of them expressed his revulsion, adding that he could not stoop to such a sin. On hearing this, his fellow elder declined to undertake the visit with him, as he knew only too well the scriptural injunction 'considering thyself, lest thou also be tempted' and obviously felt that his fellow elder was not in the right condition of heart to undertake the visit.

All the Gospel writers bear record to the boast of Peter when he vehemently affirmed:
'Though all should forsake thee, never will I.' Later, he would hear the cock crow, go out into the night, and weep bitterly, alone with his thoughts.

Good it is to read again and to remember the restoring hand of the Shepherd: (Luke 22 v 32) 'and when thou art converted, strengthen thy brethren'.

There must always be a way back and full restoration available for any of the Lord's people who turn aside from the paths of righteousness, but it does require patience, skill, and compassion on the part of the guides.

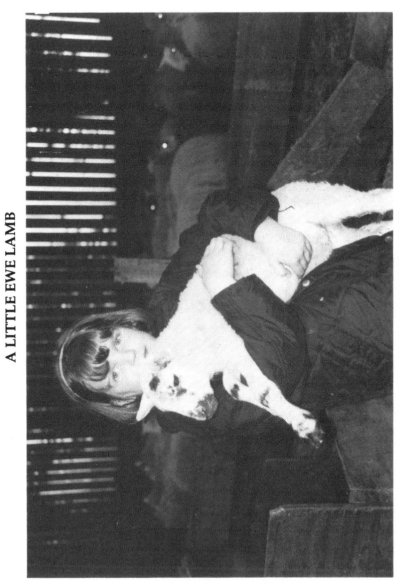

A LITTLE EWE LAMB

ONE OF THE FAMILY

THE FEEDING BOTTLE

I have admired men, attending to 'foot rot' in their sheep, who, with surgical precision and tender care, have brought about healing and restoration. It is a rather painful process, but absolutely necessary in order to have all foreign matter removed and a soothing balm applied.

Again, I have observed others, who, with a crudeness, bereft of any sympathy to the poor unfortunate animals under their charge, have treated them in a way that could only have resulted in permanent disability.

These observations, unfortunately, apply not only in secular life, but also among those who claim to have a care for the flock of God i.e. the same problems, but with different treatments.

A young girl, whom I knew, came to her elders, broken in spirit and contrite in heart, to make confession. She had run into financial problems and, in a moment of weakness, took a sum of money from her employer. Although no one found out, she had a very troubled conscience, and was about to leave the company. Caring shepherds considered the implications and:
   a) Returned the sum of money to the company marked· 'Conscience Money'.
   b) Arranged for her to repay as she could afford.
   c) Repentance with restitution brought her restoration.

Years later, the same young lady came back with her two little children to express sincere thanks for such care and confidentiality.

To use a modern expression, it is possible to: 'Crack a nut with a sledgehammer'. Some young people have developed problems with their walk, and caused offence with some trivia or other, but, alas, the knife's incision has often been too deep, exercised without skill or compassion, and, as a result, they no longer walk the pathway with us. 'Faithfulness' may be the claim but there is a very apt saying in the business world: 'It is possible to win your argument and lose your customer'. Nett result? Dead loss!

The shepherd that was introduced at the beginning of this book was certainly correct: 'You can always see more looking back, than you can looking forward'.

Peter, the great apostle, would always remember the occasions when he spoke out of turn:

In Mark 8 v 31-33, the Lord indicated that He must suffer many things and be killed, and after three days rise again. Peter said: 'Far be it from thee Lord.' He had rebuked the Lord, and was immediately rebuked himself by the Saviour: 'Get thee behind me, Satan.'

In Mark 9 v 1-7, on the Mount of Transfiguration, Peter wist not what to say and said the wrong thing, 'Let us make three Tabernacles,' only to hear the voice from heaven say: 'This is my beloved Son: hear Him.'

In Mark 14 v 27-31, there is a quote from Zechariah 13 v 7: 'I will smite the Shepherd, and the sheep shall be scattered.' Peter said: 'If I should die with thee, I will not deny thee in any wise.' (v 31)

In v 30 Jesus said: 'Verily I say unto thee, That this day, even in this night, before the cock crow twice, thou shalt deny me thrice.'

In v 72 we read that: 'Peter called to mind the word that Jesus said unto him ... And when he thought thereon, he wept.'

In Mark 16 v 7, on the morning of the resurrection, Jesus said: 'But go your way, tell his disciples and Peter that He goeth before you into Galilee.'

It is with tender love and compassion that the good Shepherd is now gathering up the flock again, after they had been scattered abroad. He is bringing the RESTORATION that was so much needed.

The good Shepherd knew that the problem had to be identified before it was possible to have it rectified.

Peter had made claims and now the Lord is bringing them out into the open.

The Gospel of John gives us details of the interview that took place between them and the precision of the words used is a study in itself (John 21 v 15-17).

When the Lord used the word 'Agape' for love, Peter knew that it carried with it the meaning of 'deep-rooted, profound, eternal love!'.

However, Peter replied with an inferior word for love, (Phileo) which carried more the meaning of 'affection, friendship, personal attachment' and was not so strong in its meaning as that which the Lord had used.

The Lord then used the inferior word (Phileo) to address Peter 'Lovest thou me?' As a result, Peter cried, 'Lord thou knowest all things.'

Like David, he now knew personally, and from bitter experience, the promise of the Lord to Israel in Hosea 14 v 4.

I WILL HEAL THEIR BACKSLIDING,
I WILL LOVE THEM FREELY.

The Lord had given Peter personal instruction in Luke 22 v 32: 'When thou art converted - strengthen thy brethren.'

The task for Peter was not fishing now but shepherding, and Peter had so much to learn about feeding lambs and shepherding sheep.

Later in his life, he was able to look back and record: 'For we were as sheep going astray; but are now returned unto the Shepherd and Bishop of our souls' (1 Peter 2 v 25).

He had learned a good deal about shepherding since the personal interview with the Lord and, therefore, was now well able to counsel others on the pathway of life.

In 1 Peter 5, he gives the shepherds the benefit of his experience:

v 2   'Feed the flock of God which is among you'.

v 3   'Be ensamples to the flock'.

v 4   'And when the chief Shepherd shall appear, ye shall receive a crown of glory that fadeth not away'.

While attending Livestock Auction Markets, at the time of the Special Lamb Sales' in various parts of Scotland, I used to watch the shepherds bringing their lambs into the sale ring with great delight and dignity. As some entered they would hand over a slip of paper to another man who was standing in the ring and observing the proceedings with keen interest.

What is happening we may ask? It was the under shepherd from one of the large estates 'Giving his Count' to the head shepherd! It is still the usual custom and practice that shepherds are both responsible and accountable for their lambs until the day in which they are sold. It is only then that they can calculate their lambing percentage with accuracy.

Peter would remind the elders that there is a chief Shepherd to whom an account must be given (1 Peter 5 v 4).

Likewise Hebrews 13 v 17 confirms:

'... for they watch (chase away sleep) for your souls, as they that must give the account.'

I discussed the health and welfare of sheep with shepherds in many parts of the country on a daily basis for many years, always aware that each had their own individual problem areas: matters that were peculiar to their own flock and for which they were personally responsible. Never, over a thirty year period, have I known any to try and resolve their neighbour's problems or treat their neighbour's sheep! Each of them knew that they should 'mind their own business'.

It is with great regret we note that this is by no means the case with so many who claim to be 'guides' among the people of God today.

Problems arise which local shepherds can identify, and possibly rectify; these matters should be kept on a flock basis and remain confidential. It is detrimental to the local church for others, who know nothing of the domestic conditions, to interfere, and make clinical judgements, for which they neither have authority nor responsibility. Much talk abounds about the 'Autonomy' of the flock, but how little of this principle is put into practice.

New diseases emerge frequently in 'the sheep world' and these can cause havoc until a remedy is found. Likewise there are pressures arising for our young people to 'conform' (be pressed into the world's mould), which were unknown to us of an older generation. I feel that it would be in order, at this point, to look at some of the problems facing young people known to me.

COUPED

IN NEED OF A SHEPHERD

'COUPED'   : 'Off their feet and on their back', and requiring the assistance of the shepherd urgently!

How many young people can you think of who have been 'couped'? Do we really understand their peer pressure? I doubt it!

Consider the following examples:

‡ A young high school boy, who is the only one in his year who does not smoke 'refeers', is continually urged to try one.

‡ University students who are ridiculed because they are among the few in their year who are not having sexual relationships with their boyfriends / girlfriends.

‡ Nurses who are being harassed to 'have a night out' with their male colleagues, some of whom are already married.

‡ Business executives who are maligned because they will not 'cook the books' or 'cut the corners' in their business transactions.

‡ Secretaries who will not 'compromise', 'tell white lies', or 'cover up' for their directors.

I mentioned some of the above situations on one occasion at a public meeting and some of my own age group thought I had gone over the top.

However, I was approached immediately by three young sisters, with tears in their eyes, who said: 'Thank you. We did not know that you knew - but it's good to know that you care.'

May I say that the above incidents are not based on conjecture but are the facts of life in our modern society.

FOOT ROT

The result of walking on contaminated marshy ground. One little experimental trip 'off the beaten track' may be taken frivolously and appear to be innocent fun, but it cannot be done without picking up the microbes that can develop and cause you to limp along the Christian pathway for life.

V 3 HE LEADETH ME IN THE PATHS OF RIGHTEOUSNESS.

We observed that the word 'leadeth' used in v 2 'He leadeth me', denotes a gentle leading. In v 3 the same phrase 'He leadeth me' appears, but this time a stronger word for 'leadeth' is used, meaning not just to 'gently lead' but to 'guide' into straight paths. In v 2 the shepherd is gently leading from the front, but in this verse, the shepherd is 'herding' the sheep into paths which they might be reluctant to enter upon, paths which could fill them with fear and anxiety.

We may think, of course, that it would be good for sheep if only they could stay in the green pastures and beside the still waters until the end of their days, but all shepherds know from experience, that this is just not practical.

There is a common saying among the sheepmen that, 'The worst enemy of a sheep is another one'. This simply means that when too many sheep stay too long in the same pasture, they develop problems. It is, therefore, essential for the shepherd to keep moving the sheep on to fresh, clean pasture, thereby taking preventive action to avert any problems developing.

In agriculture today, this type of husbandry is known as 'Rotational Grazing'. Depending on climate, stock levels, etc., it is generally known when there will be a seasonal 'rise' of parasites in any particular area, and, with experience, a good shepherd can foresee and prevent potential problems by moving the sheep on in good time. This gives the grassland time to restore itself to its former verdant freshness and lustre once again.

There are two types of treatment employed by a shepherd:

a) Prophylactic treatment - used to prevent a disease occurring.
b) Therapeutic treatment - used to treat and cure a disease.

Those who develop their skill with (a) will not require so much time with (b).

Since green pastures are sweet and more nutritious, there is the constant risk of overgrazing, as larger numbers of sheep tend to congregate than the grassland itself can naturally support. If this issue is not controlled, then cross infection of certain contagious diseases can develop rapidly and this will affect the whole flock very quickly. Generally speaking, where stock levels are low, on the higher hills, there will be cleaner pastures and less problems.

David knew that the shepherd must move the flock into 'paths of righteousness', i.e. 'carriage tracks', well known to the shepherd, although unknown to the sheep and, in v 3, no matter how reluctantly, they are guided into this way. David must have taken his sheep from lower to higher ground, knowing that it was for their ultimate good and well being. Like the sheep, David now has to place his trust and confidence in his Shepherd JEHOVAH - ROHI; even although he may not quite understand Jehovah's dealings with him, he knows from past experience: 'I shall not want'.

On a very well known Scottish island, the owners fenced off the top of the common grazing of the hill, thus depriving the crofters' sheep their usual access. After some years, the stock declined in health and became anaemic. The sheep were unthrifty and were producing very poor lambing results. This caused great concern and, as a result, a veterinary investigation took place. This revealed that the stock had suffered an acute mineral deficiency, due to the sheep having been deprived of their natural source of minerals, which had been available to them on the hill top for generations. Fortunately, the situation was rectified, and the sheep were, once again, able to get to the top of the hill and enjoy their natural habitat. Thankfully they experienced a restoration to health and produced a good lamb crop once again.

David, likewise, as a shepherd, would have taken his sheep from the green pasture of v 2 to enjoy the tablelands of v 5.

V 3 HIS NAME'S SAKE

We may not quite understand what was intended by the expression 'His name's sake', but the wise man Solomon did! And so do the shepherds.

'A good name is better than precious ointment'
(Ecclesiastes 7 v 1).
'A good name is rather to be chosen than great riches'
(Proverbs 22 v 1).

THE LAMB SALES

The annual Blackface lamb sales, which are held in many parts of Scotland, are real festive occasions and it is quite impossible to fully convey the atmosphere on paper. Shepherds, lairds and farmers lay aside their normal working clothes, don their best tweeds, and proudly carry their 'Cromag' (Gaelic for shepherd's dress crook) - made from hazel stick and rams' horn during the winter months, and often carved with ornate designs of thistles, or inscribed with names. The number of

THE FIRST OF THE LAMB SALES

A TYPICAL SHEEP MARKET

lambs gathered there could be anything from 20,000 to as much as 40,000. With all of them bleating their heart out, the noise is deafening. The feeling of expectancy runs very high, as each shepherd's flock await their turn to enter the sale ring.

As I sat down beside Donnie at the sale, I asked:
'Are you through?' -'Have you sold yet?'
'How did you get on?' - 'Did your lambs sell well?'
He replied: 'I was the first through the sale ring this morning and I am very disappointed. I'm at the bottom of the list! That gives you a very bad name.'

His whole year's work and reputation as a shepherd was at stake. 'It's not so much the money,' he said, 'but what a name! And it will be all over the papers tomorrow.'

At this point the auctioneer's voice boomed out, as he announced:
'A good pen of lambs all the way from the farm... in Glen Fruin, Dumbartonshire.'

Donnie's eyes stared at the lambs in amazement and he said: 'Do you know that area?' 'Yes,' I replied, 'very well indeed.' 'Do you know that farm?' 'Never heard of it,' I said. 'No. I should think not! Because these are my lambs!'

So off he sped to challenge the auctioneer, who was caught out with one of the little 'tricks of the trade'. The sale, which allegedly had taken place in the morning, was false. Earlier in the day, the prices were very low, with few buyers available, and the auctioneer feigned a sale with a fictitious buyer. Thinking that Donnie had gone home, he was about to sell the lambs 'again', for a much higher price, with a very handsome profit going to the clever auctioneer. My friend was more than delighted to catch the sleight of hand, have the extra profit, and, best of all, top the price of the day and retain his place among the best 'for his name's sake'.

The personal pride which shepherds have in winning trophies and in selling their stock at the top end of the market,

EXAMINATION AND TREATMENT

BEING 'HANDLED' IN THE SHEEP FANK.

rather than having it relegated to the bottom, where so often their sheep or lambs are described as 'the dross', is a real credit to their vocation and dedication.

As the apostle John writes the book of Revelation from the isle of Patmos, he sees the Lord moving among the seven golden lampstands, each on its own base. To the messenger (Angel) of each church is given an individual review:

chapter 2 v 3	EPHESUS.... for My name's sake hast laboured, and hast not fainted.
2 v 13	PERGAMOS.... thou holdest fast my name, and hast not denied my faith.
3 v 1	SARDIS.... thou hast a name that thou livest, and art dead.

It is possible that, either individually or collectively, we may be like the Sardis church; just living on a past glory or reputation and living a name which is dead.

PRIVATE AND CONFIDENTIAL

Confidence, we know, means: 'firm trust or belief; faith; trust in secrecy; a confidential communication; admission to knowledge of secrets or private affairs'. (Chambers Dictionary). It is also paramount with those who look well to their flocks that confidentiality is assured. David expresses these features to us in his lament over King Saul and over Jonathan:
'Tell it not in Gath, publish it not in the streets of Askelon; lest the daughters of the Philistines rejoice, lest the daughters of the uncircumcised triumph.' (2 Samuel 1 v 20).

On one particular day, in the course of my job, I was discussing the basic principles of immunology, and the benefits of a planned programme of preventive treatment for clostridial diseases in sheep, with a Mr. R. of Argyll. He listened intently, and in silence, with his usual caution; then

he said, 'I'm going to tell you something I've never told any-
one in my life, because I trust you.' He then poured out to me
the many problems which had plagued his flock over many
years. After further consultation and discussion with our
veterinary advisors, and with Mr. R's consent, a routine
programme of vaccination was introduced. This proved to be
most effective, eliminating his 'Black Loss' and producing better lamb crops among his flock. As a result, this led to increased
profitability for Mr. R. Every year, at the Royal Highland Show,
we met together, and he always confided in me the benefits
achieved from the vaccination programme.

On a later visit to the area, one of his neighbours was press-
ing me for information regarding Mr. R. and the reason for his
change of routine. I tried to be diplomatic and evade the
subject, but he persisted. Ultimately I said, 'Can you keep a
secret?' He replied, 'I certainly can.' 'Well so can I!', I replied
and promptly bade him goodbye.

On another occasion, as I stood at the sheep fank of a well
known breeder of black face shearling rams, I listened intently
to a discussion between the owner of the rams and his
shepherd. The owner was a most flamboyant figure at the ram
sales, often taking over from the auctioneer to eulogise on the
finer points of the ram that was about to be sold. He would
outline to all the prospective buyers the features and benefits
which they could acquire, if only they had sufficient wisdom
to purchase a ram from his flock, which had such a great
reputation among the pedigree breeders. His presentations
were most impressive, as he projected himself and his stock
in such an outstanding way.

However, as I stood on that cold wintry day, silently listening and observing, I learned the secret of the high reputation
in which he was held, and found out the reason for the 'good
name' he had achieved. Although he was the well known and

prosperous owner, it was a relatively unknown shepherd who possessed the intimate knowledge of every member of this large flock. In this case the owner appeared to know very little detail of his flock in comparison to the shepherd; he only reaped the benefit and esteem that came from another man's skill and knowledge.

What a revelation it was to listen to the shepherd as each sheep passed through his hands. There were old ewes that looked frail, weak and almost unable to walk, yet these he would set aside for special care and treatment. I wondered why?

He then briefed the owner, 'You will remember, Sir....' recounting the various prizes won for shearling rams and their lambs, which had sold for high prices over the years. Pointing to individual ewes, which had been set aside for his special attention, he would proudly say:

'That's the mother of the 1st prize winner at .... and she is the grandmother of .... which sold for £... at ....'

The in depth knowledge and recall, which the shepherd had of the flock, drew forth my greatest admiration. The message was simple, but clear. Many can bask in the limelight and publicity, while the prosperity and welfare of the flock is in the capable and conscientious hands of others, who are relatively unknown.

How true to life that many an old, and apparently unknown, sister has produced so much of value in their lives, which is overlooked by many, yet will have the prize of the 'Well done thou good and faithful servant' at the Judgement Seat of Christ.

Confidences which have been received must never be betrayed, as this could ruin a farmer's reputation when selling his stock.

PRIZE SHEARLING LAMB

THE TEUCHTER, the £50,000 lamb from Elmscleugh.
(Photographed by Douglas Low)

It is a well known fact that farmers can 'Buy in' problems that they are unable to get rid of. Therefore, care and caution must always be observed, either in secular or spiritual life, when discussing matters regarding the flock.

Some time ago, I received a telephone call from a very troubled old man, regarding serious family problems. He unburdened himself to me and asked if I thought he had taken the right course of action. In the circumstances, I felt he had no alternative, and indicated this to him, but kindly suggested that it might be better if he could confide in the local elders, as they should be in a better position to be of help. His response was, 'Definitely not, as it would be the gossip around the town before the end of the week.'

How sad, but how serious, for those who have been privy to matters regarding personnel among the flock that they should betray that trust.

TRAGIC BUT TRUE

The words of the wise man Solomon apply: 'That thou mayest regard discretion, and that thy lips may keep knowledge.' (Proverbs 5 v 2). And of Malachi 2 v 7: 'For the priest's lips should keep knowledge.'

As mentioned earlier, increasing pressures are being brought to bear upon many of our younger people, which others may know very little about, and often fail to recognise.

Likewise, many older men and women are also experiencing modern day problems which can bring about severe depression:

‡ Threats of redundancy and unemployment.

‡ Pressure to meet ever increasing targets in the business world.

‡ High cost of living, bringing with it financial worries.

‡ Serious marital problems with families.

A friend of mine met a member of the 'church of Satan' while travelling, and, in conversation, the Satanist conveyed that his 'church' had prayer sessions! My friend asked, 'What do you pray for?' His reply was: 'The disruption of Christian marriage.'

WHAT A CHALLENGE!

Do we ever engage in intense supplication before the Throne of Grace for the preservation of Christian marriage for both young and old alike?

Is there an awareness that there are real problems with many in these areas, who are part of our fellowship?

How many couples do you know of who have broken up during the past years, with devastating effect on the children?

Is there a shepherd in the midst, where the flock can turn to for confidential guidance?

Can we observe attitudes amongst the young of the flock that are symptomatic of distress or anxiety?

A comment made recently by a young person about his elders was: 'O they are all very nice, but they think Queen Victoria is still on the throne; they do not understand our problems.'

Perhaps we may feel the remark was rather facetious, but if that is their genuine feeling, shepherds should take note.

Reference has already been made of the partnership which had developed between the older man, Moses, and his successor, Joshua. It is important to notice how this concord developed from the Meribah 'incident', at a time when the people were murmuring and complaining against Moses, and his leadership. The nation of Amalek, who were descendants of Esau, were always trying to impede the progress of the people of God, and exploit any situation which would hinder them, as they made their way towards the promised land of Canaan. Deuteronomy 25 v 17-18: 'Remember what Amalek did unto thee by the way, when ye were come forth out of Egypt; how he met thee by the way, and smote the hindmost of thee, even all that were feeble behind thee, when thou wast faint and weary; and he feared not God.'

Exodus 17 v 8-16:
'And Moses said unto Joshua. Choose us out men, and go out, fight with Amalek: tomorrow I will stand with the rod of God in mine hand.'
v 11 When Moses held up his hands.: Israel prevailed.
When Moses' hands fell down. : Amalek prevailed.
v 12 When Moses' hands became heavy, Aaron and Hur sat him on a stone and supported them until the end of the day.

The illustration is most applicable for us today:

'.... your adversary the devil, as a roaring lion, walketh about, seeking whom he may devour.' (1 Peter 5 v 8)

Younger people are often struggling against Satanic forces in the valley of our world, and sadly many have fallen prey to his devices. They are victims of the 'Amalek world' of today.

Are there those praying and supporting, with 'Uplifted hands on the mount' for their preservation and victory? 1 Timothy 2 v 8: 'I will therefore that men pray everywhere, lifting up holy hands, without wrath and reasoning.' The 'lifting up of holy hands', of course, is in relation to prayer. It is not to be interpreted as a literal statement implying a physical action but rather should be seen as metaphorical, as in Hebrews 12 v 12: 'Lift up the hands that hang down, and the feeble knees.'

OUTCOME OF THE CONFLICT WITH AMALEK:

'Write this for a memorial in a book, and rehearse it in the ears of Joshua: ...

And Moses built an altar, and called the name of it:

JEHOVAH - NISSI: 'Jehovah my Banner" (Exodus 17 v 14-15).

It would be good for our day, if our younger people had the daily assurance that, despite the pressures of the day, there were those who were remembering them in prayer at the Throne of Grace: that they would find grace to help in every time of need, and, as the Lord commanded Moses, young people should also be given credit wherever it is due.

Chapter Four

HIS PRESENCE AND PROTECTION

PSALM 23

❖

JEHOVAH - SHAHMMAH

The Lord is There

❖

Verse Four
Yea, though I walk through the valley of the shadow of death, I will fear no evil for thou art with me; thy rod and thy staff they comfort me.

Chapter Four

$\mathcal{H}$IS $\mathcal{P}$RESENCE
AND $\mathcal{P}$ROTECTION

PSALM 23 VERSE FOUR

Yea, though I walk through the valley of the shadow of death, I will fear no evil for thou art with me; thy rod and thy staff they comfort me.

It has been suggested, by those who have studied the topography of the region which David lived in, that 'the valley of the shadow' was a particular geographical location which David's sheep would have had to pass through, and in which there were many predators.

In 1 Samuel 13 v 18, we read of the 'Valley of Zeboim' and we learn from the scholars that it was a deep ravine East of Michmash, known as 'The Valley of Hyenas'.

In our own land, we may picture a valley as having open hills and a gentle river, but in the east it is rather different.

While travelling from Jerusalem to Jericho, the deep ravines are awesome, and it is very easy to understand the parable the Lord told of thieves waiting in the shadows to plunder the traveller. (Luke 10 v 25-37).

I have reproduced below an interesting commentary made on this verse by an old Basque Sheepherder named Fernando d'Alfonso. The commentary was taken from an article entitled 'The Basque Sheepherder and the Shepherd Psalm'. (Condensed from the National Wool Grower by James K. Wallace):

'There is an actual valley of the shadow of death in Palestine, and every sheepherder from Spain to Dalmatia knows of it. It is south of the Jericho Road leading from Jerusalem to the Dead Sea and is a narrow defile through a mountain range. Climatic and grazing conditions make it necessary for the sheep to be moved through this valley for seasonal feeding each year.'

'The valley is four and a half miles long. Its side walls are over 1,500 feet high in places and it is only ten or twelve feet wide at the bottom. Travel through the valley is dangerous, because its floor, badly eroded by cloud bursts, has gullies seven or eight feet deep. Actual footing on solid rock is so narrow in many places that sheep cannot turn around and it is an unwritten law of shepherds that flocks must go up the valley in the morning hours and down towards the eventide, lest flocks meet in the defile. Mules have not been able to make the trip for centuries, but sheep and goat herders from earliest Old Testament days have maintained a passage for their stock.'

'About half way through the valley the walk crosses from one side to the other at a place where the path is cut in two by an eight foot gully. One section of the path is about 18 inches higher than the other; the sheep must jump across it. The shepherd stands at this break and coaxes or forces the sheep to make the leap.'

'If a sheep slips and lands in the gully, the shepherd's rod is brought into play. The old-style crook is encircled around a large sheep's neck or a small sheep's chest, and it is lifted to safety. If a more modern narrow crook is used, the sheep is caught about the hoofs and lifted up to the walk.'

'Many wild dogs lurk in the shadows of the valley looking for prey. After a band of sheep has entered the defile, the leader may come upon such a dog. Unable to retreat, the leader 'baas' a warning. The shepherd, skilled in throwing his staff, hurls it at the dog and knocks the animal into the washed-out gully where it is easily killed. Thus the sheep have learned to fear no evil even in the valley of the shadow of death, for their master is there to aid them and protect them from harm.'

I feel that it would, therefore, be in keeping with the context to say that David had travelled in similar routes with his sheep, and that he is now relating this to his own experience.

Oftentimes, he had hidden himself in the natural valleys, living in the shadow of death, pursued relentlessly by the jealous King Saul or by his rebellious son, Absalom:

'For the King of Israel is come out to seek a flea, as when one doth hunt a partridge in the mountains.' (1 Samuel 26 v 20).

'I am like a pelican of the wilderness: I am like an owl of the desert. I watch, and am as a sparrow alone upon the housetop.' (Psalm 102 v 6-7)

Job, in his book, makes several references to the 'shadow of death' and by them would certainly indicate the literal article of death and the fear which it can impart:

'For the morning is to them even as the shadow of death: if one know them, they are in the terrors of the shadow of death.' (Job 24 v 17)

Personally, however, death seemed to hold no terror for Job, as is evident in his words in Job 19 v 25-26:

'For I know that my Redeemer liveth, and that he shall stand at the latter day upon the earth: And though after my skin worms destroy this body, yet in my flesh shall I see God.'

V 4   I WILL FEAR NO EVIL: FOR THOU ART WITH ME;

David has 'no fear of evil'; such is his confidence in the Shepherd. He knows from experience that there is a way through the valley, and that the valley is a shadow: he is being directed in the carriage tracks of righteousness and it is all 'for His name's sake'.

In v 4 David is seen walking with Jehovah, his Shepherd, under his care and protection. In the book of Genesis we read that the Lord God walked in the garden, but Adam and Eve hid themselves among the trees because of their sin. In spite of Adam and Eve's failure, there are others whose names are recorded in the Bible who 'walked with God', notwithstanding the very dark conditions of the day in which they lived.

ENOCH:	Genesis 5 v 22	UNGODLY DEEDS - HARD SPEECHES
NOAH:	Genesis 6 v 1-12	WICKEDNESS - CORRUPTION
ABRAHAM:	Genesis 17 v 1	BABEL - SODOM

What reward was theirs as we find each of them recorded in the Royal Genealogy of our Lord Jesus in the Gospel of Luke chapter 3 v 31-37.

A CLOSER EXAMINATION

ON THE HILL TOP

V 4 THY ROD AND THY STAFF THEY COMFORT ME.

One never sees a shepherd without his staff while tending sheep. It provides him with balance and support when moving in steep, difficult terrain. It is also used to catch a sheep or lamb when a closer examination by hand has become necessary.

I have a very special memento which was given to me by a shepherd some years ago i.e. 'a shepherd's crook'. This was his personal token of appreciation to me for a favour rendered. I never fully appreciated its true value to a shepherd, until one particular occasion when I put it into use.

It was an annual event for us to join with the young people of our Bible class for a day's outing and, on this occasion, the objective was to climb Ben Lomond (3,192 ft / 974m). As we commenced the ascent, I was being teased. I had taken the staff with me and some were saying, 'You are like old Jacob, leaning on his staff.' Quickly, the happy group scampered past me and disappeared out of sight, only to shout on passing, 'We'll see you at the top!' (Poor old boy). I plodded on slowly, with staff in hand, until I had reached around the 2,000 ft mark. I saw the group descending, but looking rather dismal. 'How was it at the top?', I asked, and all began to make excuse! 'We didn't make it. It was too rough, steep and dangerous.'

Ultimately, I reached the top of Ben Lomond, tired and thirsty, but satisfied that I had achieved a boyhood ambition.

Many and often were the occasions when I had travelled the roads below, but now I was looking from a different perspective, with awe and wonder, at the majestic beauty of our Bonnie Scotland.

The clear, blue skies afforded perfect vision of the nearby mountains of Stirling, Dumbarton, Argyll and Perth, and, in the distance, the grandeur of Ben Nevis (4,406 ft / 1,343m) was evident, with the Cuillin hills of the Isle of Skye visible, as a background, on the western coast.

The exquisite beauty of such a scene and its impact on the soul has been so well expressed by Stuart K. Hine in his hymn of praise:

'HOW GREAT THOU ART'

O Lord my God! When I in awesome wonder
Consider all the worlds Thy hands have made,
I see the stars, I hear the rolling thunder,
Thy power throughout the universe displayed.

Refrain.
Then sings my soul, my Saviour God to Thee;
How great Thou art, how great Thou art!
Then sings my soul, my Saviour God to Thee;
How great Thou art, how great Thou art!

When through the woods and forest glades I wander
And hear the birds sing sweetly in the trees;
When I look down from lofty mountain grandeur
And hear the brook and feel the gentle breeze,

And when I think that God, His Son not sparing,
Sent Him to die, I scarce can take it in;
That on the cross, my burden gladly bearing,
He bled and died to take away my sin;

When Christ shall come with shout of acclamation
And take me home, what joy shall fill my heart!
Then I shall bow in humble adoration and there proclaim,
My God, how great Thou art!

At the top, I observed that the ground around me was quite wet, and when I traced the moisture to its source, I found a spring of water at the summit of Ben Lomond! It was an experience never to be forgotten as I drank of the pure, clear, cool waters to quench my grateful, thirsty soul.

Reluctantly, I left the panoramic scene behind and returned to meet the anxious enquirers. 'Did you make it to the top?' they asked. 'Yes, I did,' I replied. 'How did you manage to climb over the steep places?' etc. etc. It was then they understood the secret of my success: 'the shepherd's staff'. This had provided me with the necessary balance over the rough terrain, and supported me when, otherwise, I would have fallen.

David knew all about this support while tending his own sheep.

The rod was like a club, as used in the East, and proved an excellent weapon when used against the wild animals that were around in the days of which David was writing.

Comfort, drawn from the support and security provided by the Lord's 'staff' and 'rod', is the delightful word of which the Psalmist writes.

When the apostle Paul answered the question which had been troubling the Corinthian believers as to how the dead were to be raised, he revealed to them a 'mystery' which they had not known before: 'We shall not all sleep, but we shall all be changed, in a moment, in the twinkling of an eye, at the last trump: for the trumpet shall sound, and the dead shall be raised incorruptible, and we shall be changed. (1 Corinthians 15 v 51-52)

He also outlined the truth of the Lord's Coming for His people to the Thessalonians and added: 'Wherefore comfort one another with these words.' (1 Thessalonians 4 v 18) How consoling for them, and for us, to know that the word 'comfort' means 'to call to one's side at a time of need'.

While all of this Psalm has had great significance in the natural and historical setting which we have considered, what countless multitudes of the flock of God have drawn comfort from it as they have approached the valley of the shadow of death at the close of the passage of life. Their experience, like David's, has been to hear the word of the Good Shepherd:

'I will never leave thee, nor forsake thee. So that we may boldly say, the Lord is my helper, and I will not fear what man shall do unto me.' (Hebrews 13 v 5-6)

'When thou passest through the waters, I will be with thee; and through the rivers, they shall not overflow thee.' (Isaiah 43 v 2)

The carriage tracks of righteousness, through the valley of Life, may be deep and often long, as they were in the experience of Job, but O for the grace and confidence to say:

'Though he slay me, yet will I trust in him.' (Job 13 v 15)

EVEN THOUGH I PASS THROUGH THE VALLEY: I WILL NOT FEAR

In my lifetime I have been privileged to witness two wonderful examples of this personal confidence.

The first occasion was when I stood by the bedside of my father in his last few hours of life. Although in severe pain, as a result of coronary thrombosis, he lifted up his hand and quoted Phillipians 3 v 21: 'Who shall change our vile body, that it might be fashioned like unto his glorious body...' and also Job 13 v 15: 'Though he slay me, yet will I trust in him...'

The second occasion was when my wife and I visited a very close friend who was suffering under a terminal illness and had been given only a short time to live. Before visiting her, we anxiously discussed what we could say in the circumstances that would either be meaningful or comforting.

On arrival, our anxiety was banished by the cheerful and confident manner with which she discussed her illness and the inevitable outcome.

In due course, her husband telephoned to say that she had been called home peacefully and requested if I would share in her funeral service. My initial response was to decline, as I felt I would be too emotionally involved, until he advised me that it had been her specific request for me to do so.

She had confidently and quietly made every detail of her arrangements, and passed through the 'valley of the shadow of death', knowing the comfort of the Lord who had redeemed her.

Chapter Five

ENEMIES SUBDUED :
FULLNESS OF JOY
AND PROVISION

PSALM 23

❖

JEHOVAH - NISSI

The Lord is My Banner

❖

Verse Five

*Thou preparest a table before me in the presence
of mine enemies: thou anointest my head with oil;
my cup runneth over.*

FRESH PASTURES

MOVING TO HIGHER GROUND
(Photograph by Douglas Low)

Chapter Five

ENEMIES SUBDUED:
FULLNESS OF JOY AND PROVISION

PSALM 23 VERSE FIVE

Thou preparest a table before me in the presence of mine enemies: thou anointest my head with oil; my cup runneth over.

❖

The shepherd...   (v 1)
has taken the sheep from the green pastures...   (v 2)
guided them in carriage tracks...   (v 3)
through the valley of the shadow of death...   (v 4)
and prepared a table...   (v 5)

It is common practice in highland areas for shepherds to send their ewe hoggs to lower pastures during the winter months, in order to develop the ewes' growth and strength before they come into the breeding stock.

In the spring time, it is amazing how the sheep jump for joy on their return to the home farm, and immediately make their way back to the 'heft' on which they were born. In the autumn, they are then put to mate with selected rams, after which they become known as gimmers.

A TABLE PREPARED

Earlier we observed that the shepherd created the right condition for the sheep to lie down; now we see he has prepared a table and has done this in the presence of the enemies.

Good management will usually make some kind of provision for the return of the ewe hoggs to their regular grazing area, wherever it is possible or practical. This means re-seeding, fertilising, draining, etc. to improve the pastures. This type of land restoration becomes obvious on many upland farms when you can see, in the distance, a beautiful patch of green grass which has been treated, in contrast to the rough barren pastures on either side.

Table lands, which are high and flat areas, located in many parts of the world, produce excellent grazing and result in quality stock. All are aware, of course, that the table indicates a place of provision and of friendship, not a place to which enemies are invited or welcomed.

We will note that the table is prepared in the presence of the enemies, not in their absence. Enemies will always be with us until the end of the journey and the last enemy to be destroyed is Death.

It has been said: 'Courage is not Fear absent: Courage is Fear Conquered.' The 'I will not fear' of v 4 was due to the 'Thou art with me' in the same verse. David was aware of protection. Now provision is also there, and all the enemies are subdued in his presence.

THE PRESENCE OF THE ENEMIES

Foxes present a difficult problem in the highlands as they make their dens among the rocks. In lower ground, they hide in the woods, and are a little easier to track down.

In the past, it was relatively easy to poison or trap a fox, but present day legislation has banned the use of poisons and traps, and this has caused a lot of difficulty for those who desire to keep foxes under control.

The Lord Jesus said of Herod: 'Go ye, and tell that fox.' (Luke 13 v 32)

How appropriate were these words uttered by the Saviour.

A shepherd I was visiting was about to phone the police to report vandalism and slaughter among his young lambs, when 'old Tom', the gamekeeper, arrived to examine the carcases. 'Nae need tae bother wi the police, it's a fox,' he confidently asserted. Each had been killed in the same peculiar way: a clean cut from the neck to the belly of the lamb, with tongue, heart, liver and stomach removed. Tom then explained that, somewhere in the area, a vixen had died, and the male fox had been left with the task of rearing unweaned cubs; ingeniously the fox had been extracting the inwards of the lambs, keeping their stomachs whole in order to preserve the milk which they had in their stomachs, chewing the more edible parts such as the tongue, heart and liver and feeding the cubs with the milk from the lambs' stomachs. It was confirmed later that someone in the area had shot at a fox, but he was not sure if he had killed it.

In Glenlochay, Perthshire, a foxes' lair was found, containing the remains and feathers of prize ducks. This was rather a mystery, as no one around kept ducks. It was eventually discovered that the foxes had killed and carried them from ten miles away; they had never killed or maimed in their own glen!

Golden eagles are also a threat as they can prey on very young lambs in the springtime, and since they are a protected species, they can present problems in the more remote areas of our country.

The different interests of shepherds, gamekeepers and conservationists are continually at variance.

Other birds of prey, such as hooded crows etc., can be shot at will, but they can still prove a menace to sheep if the sheep are caught by thorns, couped or lying sickly.

Shepherds must always be looking upward for the tell tale signs of birds hovering in the air, or other indicators among the flock, which would give warning of trouble ahead.

I was suprised, on one occasion, to see a shepherd appear from his home with a double barrel shot gun under his arm. I asked, 'Where are you heading with the gun?' He replied, 'Trouble on the hill - there's a fox somewhere!' He scanned the hills with his binoculars for some time and then handed them to me, saying, 'Look and see.' I looked, but saw nothing unusual, until he told me to watch the sheep's 'lugs'. Then I understood their anxiety. The whole flock were on the alert, ears pricked and eyes staring, sensing a danger that was unseen by the human eye, but which had affected their flock, causing anxiety and distress and upsetting their normal peace and serenity. The vigilant observation of their keeper prevented an onslaught among them as he pursued and eliminated the predator.

Most of our Scottish shepherds would pride themselves on being a 'good shot', meaning that they are accurate with their aim when shooting at predators.

In Bible times the eastern shepherds did not have access to shot guns, but they did use their slings to hurl stones on either side of any sheep that was straying too far from the flock, or at any kind of animal that was attempting to prey upon their flock.

It was said of the chosen men of Benjamin that: '... every one could sling stones at an hair breadth, and not miss.' (Judges 20 v 16)

David certainly demonstrated his skill in this area when he slung the stone, with such deadly precision, that it struck the giant Goliath on the forehead and killed him. No doubt he had perfected this kind of expertise while tending his father's sheep on the hills.

Lions, bears, jackals and hyenas would have been the main problem in David's day, but thankfully they are not found on our sheep farms now. Flies, however, are still just as great an enemy as they were of old. Although so small, they can have a devastating effect as they carry with them death and disease, not only to the animal world, but also to human beings in many parts of the world.

FULLNESS OF JOY AND PROVISION

THOU ANOINTEST MY HEAD WITH OIL.

When travelling from Loch Lomond into Argyllshire, you will come to the old road, which is so steep it is known as the 'Rest and be Thankful'; as the name implies, that's just what travellers had to do when reaching the top of this old drovers' road.

At the top of 'the rest' there is a bridge, called Butter Bridge, which leads to Butter Glen. I am informed from a local source that, in the past, butter was imported from Ireland and landed at Lochgoilhead. After this, the butter was taken over the roads to Butter Bridge, where it was melted down, and the sheep from the surrounding hills were then brought to have their 'head anointed with oil'. This was done in an endeavour to repel the Head Fly and to promote the healing of broken heads and damaged horns.

Two species of flies bring a succession of problems among our sheep, namely the Head Fly and the Blow Fly.

Head Flies tend to come in large numbers, first irritating and then biting into the soft tissue at the base of the horn. This causes the sheep to run about in a panic as they try to shake the flies off. In their frustration, the sheep will often run into thorn bushes. As a result, their wool becomes entangled and, without assistance from the shepherd, they perish.

The female Blow Fly, on the other hand, attacks in a different way, firstly searching out a suitable place to lay her eggs: a broken fleece, an open wound, faeces on the wool or the broken flesh around the horn which the Head Flies have caused, provide the most suitable sites for the development of the eggs into maggots. These maggots will, in turn, eat into the flesh of the animal, causing it much distress, and it is a most revolting sight to witness in any sheep or lamb.

On one occasion, one of our entomologists had given a great technical presentation on a new product that had been developed to repel flies and promote healing on broken horns. After the lecture, an old farmer stood up in reply, to say: 'You scientists are a great crowd of boys! Ye kin pit a man on the moon, but ye cannie stop a fly landin on a sheep's heid.' - Humorous but nonetheless true.

MY CUP RUNNETH OVER

Fernando d'Alfonso wrote of this verse:

'At every sheepfold there is a big earthen bowl of olive oil and a large stone jar of water. As the sheep come in for the night they are led to a gate. The shepherd lays his rod across the top of the gateway just higher than the backs of his sheep. As each sheep passes in single file, he quickly examines it for briers in the ears, snags in the cheek, or weeping of the eyes from dust or scratches. When such conditions are found, he drops the rod across the sheep's back and it steps out of line. Each sheep's wounds are carefully cleaned. Then the shepherd dips his hand into the olive oil and anoints the injury. A large cup is dipped into the jar of water, kept cool by evaporation in the unglazed pottery, and is brought out - never half full but always overflowing. The sheep will sink its nose into the water clear to the eyes, if fevered, and drink until fully refreshed.

When all the sheep are at rest, the shepherd lays his staff on the ground within easy reach in case it is needed for protection of the flock during the night, wraps himself in his heavy woollen robe and lies down across the gateway, facing the sheep, for his night's repose.'

Whenever the cup is mentioned, it is the content of the vessel and not the vessel itself that is of importance. David was anointed in his father's house as the King, even though Saul was still on the throne.

The anointing oil, mentioned in the Old Testament, was used on three ceremonial occasions for:- prophets, priests and kings.

It has been described in the following ways:-

HOLY ANOINTING OIL - OIL OF GLADNESS - PRECIOUS OINTMENT

1. It shall be a **holy anointing oil**:   Exodus 30 v 25
... neither shall ye make any like it: Exodus 30 v 32

2. God hath anointed thee with the **oil of gladness** above thy fellows: Psalm 45 v 7

3. ... how pleasant for brethren to dwell together in unity! It is like the **precious ointment**:   Psalm 133 v 2

David now fully appreciates the blessings which are his:

Flock resting at the table	-	Enemies subdued
Head anointed with oil	-	Cup running over

His heart is just bursting with joy to be with JEHOVAH - ROHI.

Chapter Six

ALL THE DAYS OF MY LIFE

PSALM 23

❖

JEHOVAH - SHALOM

The Lord Send Peace

❖

Verse Six
Surely goodness and mercy shall follow me all the days of my life: and I will dwell in the house of the Lord forever.

Chapter Six

ALL THE DAYS
OF MY LIFE

PSALM 23 VERSE SIX

Surely goodness and mercy shall follow me all the days of my life: and I will dwell in the house of the Lord forever.

❖

We have listened to the sweet psalmist of Israel singing of his JEHOVAH - ROHI, and observed his wisdom, as the patriarch, reviewing the foot steps of the flock. Now, finally, we shall be instructed by the word of the prophet, as he looks forward to his eternal rest.

'Surely' is an affirmation of the beneficial goodness and the loving-kindness of His mercy.

The meaning of the expression 'shall follow' is that of 'one group pursuing another'. It is the same word as that used by David when he told Saul that he had come to 'hunt' a partridge in the mountains. (1 Samuel 26 v 20)

David is not now being pursued by the enemies that have been subdued at the table, but rather he is confident in the knowledge that behind him are the dual attributes of God's goodness and mercy.

This sense of dual protection was experienced in reality by the children of Israel when the angel of God and the pillar of the cloud went behind them and came between the Egyptians and them as they were being pursued by Pharaoh and 600 chosen captains with their chariots. (Exodus 14 v 19)

Looking back over life, he could recall moments both of triumph and of anguish, but now there is permanent assurance that all is well for him: life for David is no longer passing, transient or uncertain, for God's goodness and mercy shall follow him 'all the days of my life'. His prospect, at the end of this, is to 'dwell in the house of the Lord for ever'.

Shepherds, in the East, would look longingly to the end of the day when, footsore and weary, they would enter the sheepfold with its rest and safety. No doubt David, as the shepherd, is drawing a similar picture for us here.

BLACKFACE RAMS COMING HOME

THE END OF THE SEASON
(Photograph by Douglas Low)

I WILL DWELL IN THE HOUSE OF THE
LORD FOR EVER.

We may wonder what 'house' it is that David is referring to. The Tabernacle, that God instructed Moses to make according to the pattern, had long since gone, and the Temple of Solomon's Glory had not, as yet, been commissioned.

THE ARK OF THE COVENANT

In the days of Eli the priest, we learn that the Ark of the Covenant had been taken to the battle field by his wicked sons, Hophni and Phinehas, and had been captured by the Philistines. This was a tragic day for the nation of Israel and it was rightly called 'Ichabod': 'The glory hath departed'. (1 Samuel 4 v 1-21)

Later, the Ark was returned to the house of Abinadab, and it remained there for twenty years. (1 Samuel 7 v 2) It was then kept, for a little while, in the house of Obed-edom, but, although the people lamented for it, there was no one in Israel that sought its return during the reign of Saul the King.

David would have known of the instruction that God gave Moses concerning this central vessel of the Tabernacle, linking its physical presence in Israel with the promise of His presence in their midst.

'And there I will meet with thee, and I will commune with thee from above the mercy seat, from between the two cherubims which are upon the ark of the testimony...' (Exodus 25 v 22)

There are three things that marked David's life history:

1. The VOICE   2. The VOW   3. The VISION

These are all described for us by David in Psalms 132 and 133.

The VOICE	He heard this in his youth at Bethlehem.
Psalm 132 v 6:	'Lo, we heard of it at Ephratah.'
The VOW	He made this before Nathan the prophet.
Psalm 132 v 4-5:	'I will not give sleep to mine eyes, Or slumber to mine eyelids, Until I find out a place for the Lord, an habitation for the Mighty God of Jacob.'
The VISION	The Ark of the Covenant recovered.
Psalm 132 v 7-8:	'We will go into his tabernacles: We will worship at His footstool. Arise, O Lord, into thy rest; Thou, and the Ark of Thy strength.'

It was with tremendous rejoicing that David saw the Ark brought back from the house of Obed-edom and installed in the City of David, awaiting the building of the Temple, under the guidance of his son, Solomon.

THE HOUSE OF THE LORD

Although David was never permitted, in person, to see the Glory of the House, with the Ark of the Covenant installed in it, he certainly did enter into the good of it, as he records in Psalm 133:

v 1   'Behold, how good and how pleasant it is for brethren to dwell together in unity!

v 2   It is like the precious ointment upon the head, that
       ran down upon the beard, even Aaron's beard:
       that went down to the skirts of his garments;
v 3   As the dew of Hermon, and as the dew that
       descended upon the mountains of Zion:
       for there the Lord commanded the blessing,
       even life for evermore.'

While the Psalms do convey to us the past, present and future of the shepherd David's experience, they also portray the glory of Christ, as was brought to the attention of the audience, when the apostle Peter preached, after the Day of Pentecost, outlining the many prophecies of David.

How many facets of beauty there are in the delightful meditation of Psalm 23:

‡ Guidance for shepherds who tend the flock of God:
   providing, protecting, restoring and leading.

‡ Comfort and consolation for the Lord's people in their times of adversity, and in the depths of the many valleys of life, through which so many are called to pass.

‡ Courage, given by His presence, in the face of the Shadow of Death, knowing that the Shepherd is there, with His staff to provide support and bring comfort.

‡ Faith to appreciate that all enemies will be subdued and put 'under His feet'; even the last enemy of Death will be destroyed.

‡ Confidence: at the 'final gathering' of the flock, we shall be at home with the Good Shepherd.

As the Lord gathered the little flock around Him, after His resurrection, He spoke of times and seasons, and the Spirit has revealed to us details regarding the time table of God.

PAST	(Acts 1 v 1-2)	'All that Jesus began both to do and teach, until the day in which He was taken up.'
PRESENT	(Acts 2 v 34-35)	'Sit on my right hand, until I make thy foes thy footstool.'
FUTURE	(Acts 3 v 20-21)	'He shall send Jesus Christ, which before was preached unto you: Whom the heaven must receive until the times of the restitution.'

Although the sweet psalmist wrote his songs of praise at least one thousand years before the advent of our Lord Jesus, his prophecies are so accurate, that even an eye witness could not have given a better description of past, present or future events:

Psalm 22:
The CROSS

We will never be able to understand or fully appreciate the 'abandonment', until we see Him face to face.

Psalm 23:
The CROOK

We can draw comfort and strength to know 'I shall not want' so 'I shall not fear'.

Psalm 24:
The CROWN

Lift up your heads, O ye gates; and be ye lift up, ye ever-lasting doors; and the King of Glory shall come in.

We may be asked to pass through the valley of the shadow of death; better,of course, is the prospect that we may not!

1 Thessalonians 4 v 16-18:

'For the Lord himself shall descend from heaven with a shout, with the voice of the archangel, and with the trump of God: and the dead in Christ shall rise first: then we which are alive and remain shall be caught up together with them in the clouds, to meet the Lord in the air: and so shall we ever be with the Lord. Wherefore comfort one another with these words.'

THE FINAL GATHERING

And other sheep I have, which are not of this fold: them also I must bring, and there shall be one fold, and one shepherd.

At this moment of triumph, every sheep who has heard the voice of the Good Shepherd in time, will be 'gathered together' in the clouds to meet in the air, to go in and out no more.

2 Thessalonians 2 v 1:
'Now we beseech you, brethren, by the coming of our Lord Jesus Christ, and by our gathering together unto him.'

'WHAT A GATHERING'

We'll all gather home in the morning,
On the banks of the bright Jasper sea,
We'll meet the redeemed and the faithful;
What a gathering that will be!

Chorus:
What a gathering, gathering, gathering
that will be!
What a gathering, gathering,
What a gathering that will be!

We'll all gather home in the morning,
At the sound of the great Jubilee;
We'll all gather home in the morning,
What a gathering that will be!

We'll all gather home in the morning,
Our blessed Redeemer to see!
We'll meet with the friends gone before us,
What a gathering that will be.

We'll all gather home in the morning,
To sing of redemption so free;
We'll praise Him, for grace so abounding,
What a gathering that will be!

Gospel Hymn Book

The Good Shepherd, who gave His life for the sheep (John 10), was brought again from the dead as the Great Shepherd (Hebrews 13), and He will soon appear as the Chief Shepherd (1 Peter 5).

Even so, come Lord Jesus!

THE FLOCK

THE GATHERING
(Photograph by Douglas Low)

~ *There Is A Fold Whence None Can Stray* ~

There is a fold whence none can stray,
And pastures ever green,
Where sultry sun, or stormy day,
Or night is never seen.

There is a shepherd living there,
The firstborn from the dead,
Who tends with sweet, unwearied care
The flock for which He bled.

There congregate the sons of light,
Fair as the morning sky,
And taste of infinite delight
Beneath their Saviour's eye.

Their joy bursts forth in strains of love,
In one harmonious song,
And through the heavenly courts above
The echoes roll along.

O may our faith take up that sound,
Though toiling here below!
Midst trials may our joys abound,
And songs amidst our woe.

Until we reach that happy shore,
And join to swell their strain,
And from our God go out no more,
And never weep again.

By John East

Psalm 23

~ *The Psalter* ~

The Lord's my Shepherd, I'll not want:
He makes me down to lie
In pastures green; He leadeth me
The quiet waters by.

My soul He doth restore again,
And me to walk doth make
Within the paths of righteousness,
E'en for His own Name's sake.

Yea, though I walk in death's dark vale,
Yet will I fear none ill;
For Thou art with me, and Thy rod
And staff me comfort still.

My table Thou hast furnished
In presence of my foes;
My head Thou dost with oil anoint,
And my cup overflows.

Goodness and mercy all my life
Shall surely follow me;
And in God's house for evermore
My dwelling-place shall be.

Scottish Psalter 1650

Psalm 23

~ *A Scottish Shepherd's Version* ~

Wha is my Shepherd, weel I ken,
The Lord Himsel' is He;
He leads me whaur the girse is green
An' burnies quaet that be.

Aft times I fain astray wad gang.
An' wann'r far awa',
He fin's me oot, He pits me richt,
An' brings me hame an' a.

Tho' I pass through the gruesome cleagh,
Fin' I ken He is near,
His muckle crook will me defen';
Sae I hae nocht to fear.

Ilk comfort whilk a sheep could need,
His thoctfu' care provides
Tho' wolves an' dogs may prowl aboot,
In safety me He hides.

His guidness an' His mercy baith,
Nae doot will bide wi' me,
While faulded on the fields o'time
Or o' eternity.

Anonymous

GLOSSARY

SHEEP

EWE	A mature female sheep.
LAMB AT FOOT	Unweaned lambs of either sex.
EWE HOGG	A young female, between weaning and first shearing.
GIMMER	Weaned female: matured to breed.
SHEARLING RAM	A male of the first year.
RUMINANT	An animal which chews the cud.

FARMING

GATHERINGS	Gathering of flock for treatment.
HANDLING	When stock is physically handled.
STALKER / SHEPHERD	Dual responsibility for sheep and deer farming.
CROFTER	Highland farmer with small farm.
SHEEP FANK	Sheep fold.
HEFT	Natural division of hill farm.
RUMINATING	Chewing the cud.
COUPED	Off their feet and on their back.
VIXEN	A female fox.
DIPPING	Being dipped in insecticide.
SHEARING	Wool being removed annually.
CROMAG	Gaelic for a shepherd's crook.

DISEASES

ECTO-PARASITE	A parasite that lives on the exterior of the host.
ENDO-PARASITE	A parasite that lives on the interior of the host.
PROPHYLACTIC	Preventive treatment.
THERAPEUTIC	Curative treatment.
ANAEMIC	Blood deficient: undernourished.
BLACK DISEASE	Caused by migrating liver fluke.
BLACK LOSS	Deaths of an unknown nature.
NEMATODES	Thread like worms.
FOOT ROT	Microbes invading the soft tissue of the hoof, causing lameness.

OTHERS

C.V.	Record of work experience.

BIBLIOGRAPHY

The Shepherd's Guide	H.M. Stationery Office J. Russell Greig Phd., M.R.C.V.S., F.R.S.E.
Strong's Exhaustive Concordance	James Strong S.T.D., L.L.D.
Thayer's Greek - English Lexicon	Joseph H. Thayer
Hebrew - Chaldee Lexicon	H. F. W. Gesenius
Old Testament Hebrew Word Studies	William Wilson
Word Studies in Greek N.T.	Kenneth S. Wuest
Greek Concordance of N.T.	George V. Wigram
Newberry Bible	Thomas Newberry
National Wool Growers	James K. Wallace
Chambers Dictionary	Chambers

PHOTO ACKNOWLEDGEMENT

I would like to express my sincere thanks to
Mr J. Maxwell of Fintry for giving me permission to
photograph his flock.
(pp 36,37,55,62,76)

∼ *A Sheep ... Not A Lamb!* ∼

'Twas a sheep, not a lamb, that went astray
In the parable Jesus told;
'Twas a grown up sheep that wandered away
From the ninety and nine in the fold;

And out on the hilltop, and out in the cold,
'Twas a sheep that the good shepherd sought;
And back to the flock and back to the fold
'Twas a sheep that the good shepherd brought.

Now why should the sheep be so carefully fed
And cared for even today?
Because there is danger if they go wrong
They will lead the lambs astray.

The lambs will follow the sheep you know
Wherever they wander, wherever they go.
If the sheep go wrong it will not be long
Till the lambs are as wrong as they.

So still with the sheep must we earnestly plead
For the sake of the lambs today;
If the lambs are lost what a terrible cost
The sheep will have to pay.

Author Unknown